HEMP HOROSCOPES

Hemp Horoscopes

Cosmic Insights & Earthly Healing

Matthew Petchinsky

Apophis Enterprises LLC

1

Hemp Horoscopes: Cosmic Insights & Earthly Healing
By: Matthew Petchinsky

Introduction 1A

Astrology has been a fascination for thousands of years, there are many different versions of it and it has had the hearts and mind of man in every culture on Earth, since mankind was primitive Caveman in a cave to Egyptian to modern man. Astrology is engrained in our DNA. Please enjoy this book.

Hemp has been used for thousands of years, it is ingrained in our DNA as well. Take a deep look into a mixture of Hemp and Astrology.

Introduction 2B

Welcome to "Hemp Horoscopes: Cosmic Insights & Earthly Healing," a guide that intertwines the ancient wisdom of astrology with the natural healing properties of hemp. This book is designed for those who seek a deeper understanding of themselves and the universe, and for those who are curious about how the natural world can enhance our physical, mental, and spiritual well-being.

The Stars and Ourselves: The Role of Astrology in Personal Growth

Astrology, the study of the movements and relative positions of celestial bodies interpreted as having an influence on human affairs and the natural world, has been a source of guidance and insight for thousands of years. Beyond the sun signs, astrology offers a nuanced map of our personalities, our potential, and our paths in life. It helps us to understand our strengths, challenges, and the timing of our actions. In this book, we delve into how astrology can serve as a tool for personal growth and self-understanding, helping us to navigate life's ups and downs with greater awareness and resilience.

-

Hemp: A Journey Through History and Healing

Hemp, a plant with a history as rich and varied as astrology, has been cultivated by humans for thousands of years, used for fiber, food, and medicine. Despite its long history of beneficial uses, hemp has been misunderstood and, at times, misrepresented. This book aims to demystify hemp, presenting its true nature as a versatile and healing plant. We will explore its historical significance, its myriad uses, and the common misconceptions that have clouded its perception in modern times.

The Cosmos and Natural Healing: A Symbiotic Relationship

There exists a profound connection between the cosmos and natural healing practices. Just as the movements of the planets and stars can guide us toward personal growth, the Earth provides us with natural remedies and healers. Hemp is among these gifts, offering healing properties that align with our bodies and spirits. By understanding the cosmic influences on our lives, we can better harness the healing power of hemp, choosing strains and practices that resonate with our astrological makeup.

Navigating This Book: A Path to Insights and Healing

"Hemp Horoscopes: Cosmic Insights & Earthly Healing" is more than a guide; it's a journey through the zodiac, pairing each sign with specific hemp strains and products that harmonize with astrological energies. Whether you're an Aries seeking vitality and courage or a Pisces in search of soothing and spiritual connection, this book offers tailored insights to enhance your well-being.

As you turn these pages, you'll learn how to use astrology and hemp in tandem for personal insight and healing. From understanding your sun sign's unique characteristics to discovering the perfect hemp strain that aligns with your astrological profile, this book provides a comprehensive approach to holistic health and self-discovery.

Let us embark on this journey together, exploring the stars above and the earth below, in search of balance, healing, and a deeper connection to the cosmos.

Part 1: Astrological Foundation

-
-
-
-
-
-
-
-
-
-
-
-
-
-
-
-
-
-
-
-
-

Chapter 1: The Zodiac Signs

Astrology provides us with a celestial roadmap, offering insights into our character, preferences, and potential. At the heart of astrology are the 12 zodiac signs, each associated with a specific segment of the sky and a unique set of qualities. These signs are grouped into four elements—Fire, Earth, Air, and Water—each adding a layer of depth to our understanding of the signs' dynamics and influences.

Fire Signs: Aries, Leo, Sagittarius

- Aries (March 21 - April 19): The first sign of the zodiac, Aries, is known for its fiery energy, courage, and initiative. Aries individuals are natural leaders, passionate and determined, always ready to blaze new trails.
- Leo (July 23 - August 22): Leos possesses a royal aura, exuding confidence, creativity, and charisma. They are generous, warm-hearted, and seek to express their individuality and power.
- Sagittarius (November 22 - December 21): The adventurers of the zodiac, Sagittarians are known for their love of exploration, their optimistic outlook, and their quest for truth and knowledge.

Earth Signs: Taurus, Virgo, Capricorn

- Taurus (April 20 - May 20): Taurus individuals are grounded, practical, and reliable. They have a profound connection to the physical world, valuing stability, comfort, and sensory pleasures.
- Virgo (August 23 - September 22): Virgo is the sign of meticulousness, efficiency, and a deep sense of duty.

Virgos are analytical, detail-oriented, and seek to improve themselves and their surroundings.
- Capricorn (December 22 - January 19): Capricorns are known for their discipline, ambition, and resilience. They are patient and strategic, with a long-term view towards success and achievement.

Air Signs: Gemini, Libra, Aquarius

- Gemini (May 21 - June 20): Geminis are the communicators of the zodiac, known for their intellect, curiosity, and versatility. They thrive on variety, exchange of ideas, and social interactions.
- Libra (September 23 - October 22): Libra is the sign of balance, harmony, and relationships. Libras seek fairness and beauty in all things and are diplomatic, charming, and sociable.
- Aquarius (January 20 - February 18): Aquarians are the visionaries, valued for their originality, independence, and humanitarian spirit. They are innovative, forward-thinking, and committed to making the world a better place.

Water Signs: Cancer, Scorpio, Pisces

- Cancer (June 21 - July 22): Cancers are deeply intuitive and emotional, valuing home, family, and emotional security. They are nurturing, protective, and have a strong connection to their past and heritage.
- Scorpio (October 23 - November 21): Scorpios are known for their intensity, depth, and passion. They are determined, powerful, and seek to understand life's mysteries and complexities.

: <u>Pisces (February 19 - March 20):</u> Pisces are the dreamers and mystics of the zodiac, characterized by their empathy, creativity, and spiritual depth. They are compassionate, imaginative, and sensitive to their environment and the feelings of others.

Each zodiac sign offers a unique lens through which we can view ourselves and the world. Understanding the characteristics and elements of your sign can provide valuable insights into your personality, preferences, and the natural rhythms that guide your life. As we delve into the healing properties of hemp in the chapters to come, we'll explore how this ancient plant aligns with the energies of each zodiac sign, offering personalized paths to balance, wellness, and self-discovery.

-
-
-
-
-
-
-
-
-
-
-
-
-
-
-
-
-
-
-

Chapter 2: Planets and Houses- The Framework of The Cosmos.

Astrology is not only the study of the stars but also the planets and houses that influence our lives. These celestial bodies and sectors offer a more detailed and personalized astrological analysis, going beyond sun signs to reveal the complexities of personality, life events, and potential paths. This chapter delves into the roles of the planets and the astrological houses, providing a foundational understanding of how they interact with the zodiac signs to guide our journey through life.

The Planets: Celestial Bodies of Influence

Each planet in astrology represents a different aspect of life, reflecting our desires, actions, and the various facets of our personality. Here is an overview of the primary astrological planets and their significances:

- **Sun**: Represents our core identity, ego, and the essence of who we are.
- **Moon**: Governs our emotions, instincts, and unconscious needs.
- **Mercury**: Rules communication, intellect, and how we process and exchange information.
- **Venus**: Associated with love, beauty, and what we value in relationships and art.
- **Mars**: Represents our drive, energy, and how we assert ourselves and pursue our goals.
- **Jupiter**: Signifies expansion, luck, and our philosophical outlook on life.
- **Saturn**: Reflects discipline, responsibility, and challenges that lead to growth.
- **Uranus**: Symbolizes innovation, rebellion, and sudden changes that disrupt the status quo.

- **Neptune**: Governs our dreams, illusions, and connection to the spiritual and non-material realms.
- **Pluto**: Represents transformation, power, and deep subconscious forces.

The Houses: The Stage of Life

In astrology, the houses represent different areas of life's journey, where the planets' energies play out. There are 12 houses, each corresponding to a zodiac sign, but individually mapping out the sectors of one's life:

1. **First House (House of Self)**: Identity, appearance, first impressions, and new beginnings.
2. **Second House (House of Value)**: Finances, possessions, values, and self-worth.
3. **Third House (House of Communication)**: Communication, siblings, local travel, and early education.
4. **Fourth House (House of Home and Family)**: Home, family, ancestry, and emotional foundations.
5. **Fifth House (House of Pleasure)**: Creativity, romance, children, and personal expression.
6. **Sixth House (House of Health)**: Work, health, service, and daily routines.
7. **Seventh House (House of Partnerships)**: One-on-one relationships, business partnerships, and marriage.
8. **Eighth House (House of Transformation)**: Transformation, sexuality, death, and shared resources.
9. **Ninth House (House of Philosophy)**: Higher education, travel, philosophy, and spirituality.
10. **Tenth House (House of Career)**: Career, ambition, reputation, and public image.
11. **Eleventh House (House of Friendships)**: Friendships, groups, social aspirations, and future goals.

12. <u>Twelfth House (House of the Unconscious)</u>: The unconscious, secrets, hidden enemies, and karmic debts.

The planets move through these houses as they orbit, activating different areas of our lives at different times. The position of the planets in these houses at the time of our birth offers a blueprint of our potential experiences, challenges, and growth areas.

<u>The Dance of the Cosmos</u>

Understanding the roles of the planets and houses in astrology provides us with a more nuanced view of our natal charts and life paths. These celestial factors work together, influencing our characteristics, behaviors, and the timing of events. As we explore the connection between these astrological elements and hemp in subsequent chapters, we'll discover how the planets and houses can guide us in selecting the most harmonious hemp strains and products for our personal healing and growth.

The cosmic dance of planets through the houses under the watchful eyes of the zodiac signs forms a complex, interconnected web of potential and influence. By learning to navigate this cosmic framework, we can unlock deeper insights into our personalities, relationships, and the unfolding journey of our lives.

-
-
-
-
-
-
-
-
-

Chapter 3: The Hemp Connection- A Celestial Bond

The journey through the stars and the exploration of the self through astrology find a grounding counterpart in the earthy resilience of hemp. This chapter delves into the intertwined history and spiritual connections between hemp and astrology, highlighting how this ancient plant has been a companion to humans in rituals, medicine, and the quest for understanding the cosmos.

The Historical Tapestry of Hemp

Hemp's history with humanity is as old as the stars in the sky, tracing back over 10,000 years. Cultivated for its fibers, seeds, and medicinal properties, hemp has been a staple in civilizations across the globe. From the ancient Chinese, who used hemp in their textiles and medicine, to the Egyptians, who included hemp seeds in their tombs for the afterlife, the plant has been revered for its versatility and healing powers.

In the realm of astrology, plants have always held a significant role, with each herb and plant linked to specific celestial bodies and signs. Hemp's robust nature and its ability to thrive in various conditions made it a symbol of resilience, healing, and universal connection in ancient astrological texts. Astrologers believed that hemp resonated with the energies of Saturn, the planet of discipline, responsibility, and growth through challenges. This connection underscores hemp's role in grounding and providing a foundation for spiritual and physical well-being.

Spiritual and Ritualistic Uses of Hemp

Beyond its practical applications, hemp has been intertwined with the spiritual and the mystical. Shamans and healers have used hemp in rituals to cleanse auras, protect against negative energies, and connect with the spiritual realm. The plant's ability to induce states of deep relaxation and heightened awareness made it a tool for meditation and communication with the divine.

In astrology, the practice of aligning one's life with the movements of the planets and stars is a form of spiritual attunement. Similarly, the use of hemp in rituals and healing practices is a way to align the physical body with the spiritual and cosmic energies. The integration of hemp into astrological practices can be seen as a method of harnessing the earth's gifts to enhance our understanding and connection to the cosmos.

Hemp and Astrological Healing

The medicinal properties of hemp, particularly in the form of CBD (cannabidiol), have gained recognition in modern times for their ability to alleviate pain, reduce anxiety, and support overall wellness. This resurgence echoes the ancient understanding of hemp as a healer. When viewed through the astrological lens, hemp's healing properties can be tailored to individual signs and planetary influences, offering personalized pathways to balance and health.

For instance, the calming effects of CBD can be particularly beneficial for signs prone to stress and anxiety, such as Virgos and Geminis, while the energizing aspects of certain hemp strains may invigorate the fiery nature of Aries and Leo. By considering the planetary rulerships and elemental qualities of each sign, astrologers and healers can recommend specific hemp-based remedies to align with and enhance the cosmic energies at play.

The Cosmic Cycle of Cultivation

The cultivation of hemp itself reflects a deep understanding of cosmic and natural cycles. Astrologers and farmers alike have observed the moon's phases and planetary alignments to determine the best times for planting, tending, and harvesting hemp. This practice, known as biodynamic farming, is based on the principle that the cosmos directly influences the growth and vitality of plants on Earth. By aligning hemp cultivation with astrological cycles, growers tap into the celestial power, imbuing the plant with enhanced energetic properties.

Conclusion

The bond between hemp and astrology is a testament to humanity's enduring quest to understand and harness the energies of the cosmos. Through the historical use of hemp in spiritual practices to the modern exploration of its healing properties, this versatile plant serves as a bridge between the earthly and the celestial. As we continue our journey through "Hemp Horoscopes: Cosmic Insights & Earthly Healing," we invite readers to explore the deep connections between their astrological signs and the healing power of hemp, embracing the ancient wisdom that unites the stars above with the earth below.

Part 2: Hemp Horoscopes

As we embark on a journey through the zodiac, pairing each sign with hemp strains and products that align with their unique energies, we begin with the first six signs. Each sign has its own set of needs and qualities, and hemp can be a powerful ally in enhancing health, relaxation, and spiritual well-being. Here, we explore Aries through Virgo, offering insights into how specific hemp products can support and nurture these signs.

Aries (March 21 - April 19): The Trailblazer

Energizing Strains for Initiative and Courage

- **Strain Recommendations:** Look for strains that are known for their uplifting and energizing effects, such as Sativa-dominant hybrids. These strains can enhance Aries' natural vigor and drive.
- **Product Suggestions:** CBD vape pens with citrus terpene profiles can invigorate the senses, promoting an active and lively mindset.
- **Usage Recommendations:** Aries individuals may benefit from using these energizing strains in the morning or

before embarking on new projects. They can help fuel your ambition and tackle challenges head-on.

Taurus (April 20 - May 20): The Sensualist

Grounding Hemp Products for Relaxation and Sensory Enjoyment

- : **Strain Recommendations**: Taurus individuals will appreciate strains with a rich, earthy aroma and a balanced CBD to THC ratio, offering relaxation without sedation.
- : **Product Suggestions**: Hemp-infused body oils or lotions can provide sensual pleasure, while edible products like hemp chocolates cater to Taurus' love for indulgence.
- : **Usage Recommendations**: Evening use of these grounding products can help unwind and soothe the senses, enhancing Taurus' appreciation for comfort and relaxation.

Gemini (May 21 - June 20): The Communicator

Versatile Uses of Hemp for Adaptability and Communication

- : **Strain Recommendations**: Geminis will benefit from strains that promote focus and creativity, aiding their versatile nature and enhancing communication skills.
- : **Product Suggestions**: CBD tinctures for daytime use can keep Geminis alert and engaged, while hemp tea can provide a calming effect for the mind, fostering clear communication.
- : **Usage Recommendations**: Use tinctures or teas during social events or creative endeavors to harness Gemini's adaptability and eloquence.

Cancer (June 21 - July 22): The Caregiver

Comforting Hemp Uses for Nurturing and Protection

- **Strain Recommendations:** Indica strains or those high in CBD can offer the comfort and relaxation Cancerians seek, providing a sense of protection and nurturing.
- **Product Suggestions:** CBD-infused bath bombs or salts can enhance Cancer's self-care routines, creating a sanctuary of peace and comfort in their home environment.
- **Usage Recommendations:** Evening use, especially after emotionally draining days, can help soothe the mind and nurture Cancer's soul, promoting restful sleep and emotional recovery.

Leo (July 23 - August 22): The Performer

Bold Strains for Creativity and Self-Expression

- **Strain Recommendations:** Leos will thrive with strains that spark creativity and euphoria, enhancing their natural flair for drama and self-expression.
- **Product Suggestions:** Hemp flower with a high terpene profile can stimulate the senses, while CBD-infused hair or skin products can appeal to Leo's love for personal grooming and appearance.
- **Usage Recommendations:** Use these bold strains before engaging in creative projects or social gatherings to amplify Leo's charismatic presence and creative output.

Virgo (August 23 - September 22): The Healer

<u>Healing and Purifying Hemp Applications for Health and Wellness</u>

- **<u>Strain Recommendations</u>**: <u>Virgos will appreciate strains that offer clear-headedness and are known for their healing properties, particularly those high in CBD.</u>
- **<u>Product Suggestions</u>**: <u>CBD capsules or supplements can support Virgo's health-focused lifestyle, while topical products can address physical discomfort, aligning with their need for purity and wellness.</u>
- **<u>Usage Recommendations</u>**: <u>Integrating CBD supplements into their daily wellness routine can help maintain Virgo's health and well-being, while topical applications can be used as needed for physical recovery.</u>

As we explore the unique connections between each zodiac sign and the world of hemp, it becomes clear that this ancient plant offers a vast spectrum of benefits tailored to our individual astrological energies. From the fiery ambition of Aries to the meticulous care of Virgo, hemp stands as a versatile ally in our quest for balance, health, and harmony with the cosmos.

Top of Form

As for the Products that are suggested head over to my Virtual Dispensary for a quick, Discreet shipping, you can go to: https://shift.store/sg1fan23477/retail

- -
- -
- -
- -
- -
- -

-

-

-

Chapter 5: Libra through Pisces: Aligning Hemp with the Zodiac's Second Half

Continuing our celestial journey, we now turn to the latter six signs of the zodiac, exploring how hemp can be harmonized with their distinct energies. From Libra's quest for balance to Pisces' depth of imagination, each sign reveals unique needs and preferences that can be supported and enhanced through tailored hemp products and strains.

Libra (September 23 - October 22): The Harmonizer

Balanced Strains for Harmony and Relationships

- **Strain Recommendations**: Libras will find equilibrium with hybrid strains that offer a balance of Sativa and Indica effects, promoting both social engagement and inner peace.
- **Product Suggestions**: CBD-infused beauty products or oils can appeal to Libra's aesthetic sensibilities, while promoting harmony and relaxation.
- **Usage Recommendations**: Use balanced strains during social gatherings or when seeking to restore inner peace after discord, enhancing Libra's natural diplomacy and charm.

Scorpio (October 23 - November 21): The Mystic

Intense and Transformative Hemp Uses for Healing and Mystery

- : **Strain Recommendations:** Scorpios will resonate with potent strains that offer deep relaxation and introspection, aiding in their transformative healing processes.
- : **Product Suggestions:** High-potency CBD oils or tinctures can be used for profound emotional and physical healing, tapping into Scorpio's desire for deep, transformative experiences.
- : **Usage Recommendations:** Evening use can facilitate introspection and regeneration, supporting Scorpio's journey through personal challenges and transformations.

Sagittarius (November 22 - December 21): The Explorer

Adventurous Strains for Exploration and Philosophy

- : **Strain Recommendations:** Sativa-dominant strains that stimulate the mind and enhance creativity can complement Sagittarius' love for adventure and quest for knowledge.
- : **Product Suggestions:** Portable CBD vape pens are ideal for Sagittarians on the go, while hemp-based travel essentials can support their adventurous lifestyle.
- : **Usage Recommendations:** Use these strains and products during travels or when engaging in philosophical pursuits, enhancing Sagittarius' natural curiosity and zest for life.

Capricorn (December 22 - January 19): The Strategist

Structured Hemp Applications for Ambition and Discipline

- **Strain Recommendations:** Capricorns will benefit from strains that enhance focus and productivity, supporting their disciplined and ambitious nature.
- **Product Suggestions:** CBD capsules or edibles can provide a consistent, measured dose for daily use, aligning with Capricorn's preference for structure and reliability.
- **Usage Recommendations:** Morning or daytime use can boost Capricorn's concentration and productivity, aiding in their pursuit of professional and personal goals.

Aquarius (January 20 - February 18): The Visionary

Innovative Uses of Hemp for Uniqueness and Humanitarianism

- **Strain Recommendations:** Aquarians will be drawn to unique strains that inspire creativity and foster social connections, reflecting their innovative and humanitarian spirit.
- **Product Suggestions:** Hemp-based sustainable products or those with a focus on social impact can resonate with Aquarius' values, while CBD-infused creativity aids can spark their visionary ideas.
- **Usage Recommendations:** Use when engaging in creative projects or community initiatives, amplifying Aquarius' ability to envision and enact change.

Pisces (February 19 - March 20): The Dreamer

Soothing and Spiritual Hemp Selections for Empathy and Imagination

- : Strain Recommendations: Pisces will find solace in strains that offer deep relaxation and enhance spiritual connection, nurturing their empathetic and imaginative nature.
- : Product Suggestions: CBD-infused bath products or essential oils can provide a tranquil, immersive experience, while hemp-based art supplies can inspire Pisces' creative expression.
- : Usage Recommendations: Evening use can help unwind and foster dreamy introspection, supporting Pisces' spiritual and creative journeys.

Each of these recommendations is designed to align the distinct energies of the zodiac's latter signs with the healing and harmonizing properties of hemp. By understanding and embracing these celestial influences, individuals can select hemp strains and products that enhance their personal journey, fostering balance, growth, and well-being in alignment with the cosmos.

As for the Products that are suggested head over to my Virtual Dispensary for a quick, Discreet shipping, you can go to: https://shift.store/sg1fan23477/retail

-
-
-
-
-
-
-
-
-
-
-
-
-
-
-
-

Part 3: Hemp and The Cosmos

-
-
-
-
-
-
-
-
-
-
-
-
-

-

-

-

-

-

-

Chapter 6: Moon Phases and Hemp- Embracing the Lunar Influences

The moon, with its powerful influence over the Earth, affects not only the tides but also plant growth and human emotions. In this chapter, we explore the fascinating relationship between the moon phases and hemp — from cultivation to personal use, especially in spiritual practices. Understanding the lunar cycles can enhance our connection with hemp, whether we are growing it, consuming it for health benefits, or using it in rituals to align more closely with the natural world.

The Lunar Cycle and Hemp Cultivation

The lunar cycle, consisting of four main phases — new moon, first quarter, full moon, and last quarter — has been observed by farmers and gardeners for centuries to determine the best times for planting, tending, and harvesting crops. This practice, known as biodynamic farming, applies to hemp cultivation as well, with each phase offering different benefits:

- New Moon: The new moon marks a time of initiation and beginnings. This phase is ideal for planting hemp seeds as the gravitational pull is stronger, encouraging root growth.
- First Quarter: As the moon waxes, it's a time for growth and strength. This phase is optimal for tending to your

hemp plants, such as watering and fertilizing, to encourage vigorous growth above ground.

- **Full Moon:** The full moon's intense gravitational pull and increased moonlight promote leaf growth. It's a powerful time for infusing spiritual energy into the plants and for harvesting flowers or leaves intended for medicinal and spiritual use.
- **Last Quarter:** During the waning moon, the energy is drawing down, making it a good time to harvest roots and seeds or to prune the plants to encourage regeneration.

Hemp and Spiritual Practices by Moon Phase

Integrating hemp into spiritual practices according to the moon phases can deepen your connection to both the plant and the celestial energies.

- **New Moon Hemp Rituals:** Set intentions for the coming cycle with a CBD oil meditation, focusing on what you wish to manifest. The new moon is a time for new beginnings and setting intentions, making it a perfect time to start a new hemp-based wellness routine.
- **First Quarter:** Use this time of growth to work on personal development and challenges. A hemp tea ceremony can be a way to focus on your goals and the steps needed to achieve them, energizing your efforts with the waxing moon's momentum.
- **Full Moon:** The full moon is a time of culmination and celebration. Create a full moon bath with hemp-infused bath bombs or salts, allowing the full moon's energy to charge the water, and by extension, the hemp product, enhancing its healing properties.

∴ Last Quarter: Reflect and release. The waning moon is a time for letting go of what no longer serves you. A smudging ritual with a hemp-derived product can purify your space, helping you to release negative energies and prepare for the new cycle.

Hemp Cultivation and Consumption in Harmony with the Moon

For those cultivating hemp, aligning your practices with the lunar phases can enhance the plant's growth and potency. For consumers, integrating hemp into your spiritual practices according to the moon phases can amplify your intentions and the plant's healing properties.

This chapter invites you to consider the moon's phases in your relationship with hemp, whether you're a grower, consumer, or practitioner of spiritual rituals. By attuning to the lunar cycles, you can cultivate a deeper, more harmonious connection with hemp, tapping into ancient rhythms that have guided humans and plants alike through the ages.

Chapter 7: Planetary Alignments and Hemp Healing-Cosmic Synergies

The cosmos is a vast and dynamic tapestry, with each planetary movement and alignment holding the potential to influence life on Earth. Just as these celestial events can impact our moods, behaviors, and destinies, they can also interact with the natural world, including the plants we grow and utilize for healing. This chapter delves into the intriguing interplay between planetary alignments and hemp, exploring how these cosmic forces can enhance the healing properties of this versatile plant.

Understanding Planetary Influences

Each planet exerts a unique influence, affecting not only individuals but also the natural world, including plants. For instance:

- Sun: Vitality and Growth
- Moon: Emotional Healing and Intuition
- Mercury: Communication and Nervous System Support
- Venus: Love, Beauty, and Harmony
- Mars: Energy and Assertiveness
- Jupiter: Expansion and Prosperity
- Saturn: Discipline and Structure
- Uranus: Innovation and Change
- Neptune: Spirituality and Healing
- Pluto: Transformation and Rebirth

Aligning Hemp Cultivation with Planetary Energies

Incorporating planetary alignments into the cultivation and harvesting of hemp can potentially imbue the plants with enhanced energetic qualities. For example, planting hemp seeds during a Venus transit might accentuate the plant's ability to facilitate healing and harmony. Similarly, harvesting hemp under a Jupiter alignment could amplify its capacity to bring about expansion and prosperity in healing practices.

Enhancing Hemp Healing with Planetary Alignments

The healing properties of hemp can be aligned with specific planetary energies for targeted therapeutic effects. Here are some ways to integrate planetary influences into hemp healing practices:

- **Sun-Aligned Hemp:** Utilize hemp products during periods of strong solar energy for increased vitality and to support overall wellness.
- **Moon-Aligned Hemp:** Engage in hemp-based healing rituals during different moon phases to enhance emotional healing and intuitive insights.
- **Mercury-Aligned Hemp:** Apply hemp products for communication enhancement and nervous system support when Mercury's influence is strong.
- **Venus-Aligned Hemp:** Use hemp to nurture love, beauty, and self-care practices under the auspices of Venus.
- **Mars-Aligned Hemp:** Leverage the energy of Mars to boost the invigorating and energizing effects of hemp.

Rituals and Practices

Creating rituals around planetary alignments can deepen the connection between the individual and the cosmic forces at play. For instance, a ritual performed under a Neptune alignment, involving meditation with CBD oil, can facilitate spiritual healing and connection. Similarly, engaging in a Mars-aligned practice, such as using hemp-based products for physical activity or courage, can harness Mars' fiery energy.

Planetary Retrogrades and Hemp

Planetary retrogrades offer a time for reflection and re-evaluation. During these periods, incorporating hemp into meditative and reflective practices can help navigate the introspective energy brought about by retrogrades. For example, Mercury retrograde can be a time for introspection about communication and healing, where hemp can support this inward journey.

Conclusion

The cosmos and its planetary alignments play a significant role in the natural world and our personal healing journeys. By understanding and aligning with these celestial energies, we can enhance the therapeutic potential of hemp. This chapter invites readers to explore the synergy between planetary alignments and hemp healing, offering a holistic approach to wellness that honors the interconnectedness of the cosmos and the Earth.

<u>Chapter 8: Creating your Hemp Rituals-</u>
<u>Celestial Guidance for Everyday Life</u>

Incorporating hemp into daily or weekly rituals can create a powerful practice that aligns your personal energy with the cosmic energies at play. This chapter provides guidance on how to integrate hemp into rituals based on astrological events, allowing you to harness the celestial forces to enhance your well-being, achieve balance, and manifest your intentions.

Understanding Astrological Influences

Before diving into creating rituals, it's essential to have a basic understanding of the astrological influences that can guide your practice:

- **Sun Sign**: Your core identity, vitality, and life force.
- **Moon Phase**: Emotional currents, intuition, and subconscious desires.
- **Planetary Movements**: Specific energies and themes highlighted by the current astrological transits.

Daily Rituals with Hemp

Daily rituals can help to ground your intentions, maintain balance, and connect with the celestial energies. Consider the following practices:

- **Morning Rituals**: Start your day by setting intentions with a CBD oil meditation. Reflect on your sun sign's qualities and how you can express them throughout the day.

- **Evening Rituals**: Use a hemp-infused tea or bath to unwind and release the day's energies. Reflect on the moon's phase and its emotional guidance.

Weekly Rituals Based on Planetary Days

Each day of the week is traditionally associated with a specific planet, carrying the energy of that celestial body. Tailoring your hemp rituals to these planetary days can enhance their effectiveness:

- **Moon Monday**: Focus on nurturing and emotional healing. A CBD-infused facial or body lotion can soothe both the skin and the soul, aligning with the Moon's nurturing energy.
- **Sun Sunday**: Dedicate to vitality and self-expression. A morning hemp smoothie can invigorate your body, reflecting the Sun's life-giving energy.

Rituals for Special Astrological Events

Special astrological events, such as eclipses, retrogrades, and significant planetary transits, offer powerful opportunities for specific rituals:

- **New Moon Ritual**: A time for new beginnings. Write down your intentions on hemp paper and meditate with a hemp seed oil candle to manifest your desires.
- **Full Moon Ritual**: A time for release and culmination. Create a cleansing bath with hemp salts, focusing on releasing what no longer serves you.

Personalizing Your Rituals

To personalize your rituals, consider your astrological chart and current transits. For instance:

- : If Mars is transiting your sign, you might focus on rituals that enhance courage and action, such as using energizing hemp strains before embarking on new projects.
- : During a Venus retrograde, focus on self-love rituals, perhaps incorporating hemp beauty products into your skincare routine.

Crafting Your Ritual Space

Creating a sacred space for your rituals can enhance their impact. Consider including the following:

- : Hemp Fabrics: Use hemp fabric for your altar cloth or meditation space to bring in the grounding energy of hemp.
- : Crystals and Symbols: Incorporate crystals and symbols that resonate with the current astrological energies.

Conclusion

Creating personalized hemp rituals based on astrological events offers a dynamic way to engage with both the cosmos and the healing power of hemp. By aligning your practices with the celestial energies, you can enhance your well-being, achieve deeper spiritual connections, and manifest your intentions with greater clarity and power. Let the cosmos guide you in weaving hemp into your spiritual practice, and watch as

the alignment between the stars and this sacred plant brings
harmony and healing into your life.

Part 4: Beyond The Horizon

-
-
-
-
-
-
-
-
-
-
-
-
-
-
-
-
-

-
-
-
-
Chapter 9: The Future of Hemp and Astrology- Navigating the Cosmic Weave.

As we stand at the confluence of ancient wisdom and modern innovation, the relationship between hemp and astrology is poised for a transformative evolution. This chapter ventures into the realm of speculation, imagining the future pathways that the synergy between these two fields might explore. Drawing from trends in technology, spirituality, and societal shifts, we contemplate the potential developments that could further intertwine the cosmic influence of astrology with the earthy, healing properties of hemp.

Technological Integration in Astro-Hemp Practices

The digital age has the potential to revolutionize how we engage with hemp and astrology. Imagine apps that calculate the optimal times for taking CBD based on your astrological chart and current planetary transits. Wearable technology could monitor your biometrics and suggest specific hemp strains or products aligned with the astrological influences affecting you at any given moment. This personalized approach could elevate the efficacy of hemp in our lives, making wellness truly tailored to the individual's cosmic blueprint.

Advances in Hemp Cultivation and Astrological Farming

As our understanding of the cosmos deepens, so too could our methods of cultivating hemp. Astrological farming, an extension of biodynamic practices, might see a resurgence, with cultivators planting, tending, and harvesting hemp according to lunar and planetary alignments. This method could be further enhanced by advancements in agricultural technology, potentially leading to hemp strains that are not only astrologically aligned but also genetically optimized for specific healing properties.

The Expansion of Astrological Wellness Communities

The future could see the rise of communities and networks dedicated to exploring the intersection of hemp and astrology. These groups might host retreats, workshops, and online platforms where individuals can share experiences, insights, and discoveries. Through collective exploration, these communities could unearth new ways of integrating hemp into spiritual and wellness practices, further cementing the role of astrology in holistic healing.

Ethical and Sustainable Evolution

As society moves towards greater environmental consciousness, the cultivation and use of hemp could lead the way in sustainable practices. Astrology, with its emphasis on natural cycles and energies, could play a pivotal role in shaping these practices. We might see a push towards not only using hemp in alignment with astrological principles for personal wellness but also in ways that honor and protect the Earth. This could include everything from choosing cultivation methods that align with cosmic rhythms to using hemp products in rituals designed to heal the planet.

Global Traditions and Cross-Cultural Exchange

The global exchange of knowledge and traditions could enrich the relationship between hemp and astrology. By learning from cultures around the world that have their own unique connections to the cosmos and cannabis plants, we can expand our understanding and practices. This cross-pollination of ideas could lead to a more nuanced, diverse approach to astrological wellness, incorporating insights from Vedic astrology, Indigenous star lore, and other astrological systems alongside Western traditions.

Conclusion: A Vision for the Future

The future of hemp and astrology is as vast and varied as the night sky itself. By embracing innovation while honoring ancient wisdom, we can forge a path that enhances our connection to the cosmos and the Earth. As we navigate this journey, we remain open to the mysteries of the universe, ready to discover how the stars and this remarkable plant can guide us towards greater harmony, health, and healing. In this evolving relationship, we find not only a reflection of where we have been but also a vision for where we are headed — together, under the vast, starlit sky.

-
-
-
-
-
-
-
-

<u>Appendices</u>

<u>1.</u> <u>Glossary of Astrological Terms</u>

This glossary provides definitions for key astrological terms used throughout "Hemp Horoscopes: Cosmic Insights & Earthly Healing," offering readers a foundation for understanding the celestial language that influences our connection with hemp and the cosmos.

- <u>Ascendant (Rising Sign)</u>: <u>The zodiac sign that was rising on the eastern horizon at the moment of one's birth, representing the persona and outward appearance.</u>
- <u>Aspect</u>: <u>The angles formed by the planets in relation to one another in a natal chart, indicating how the planets' energies combine and interact.</u>
- <u>Biodynamic Farming</u>: <u>An agricultural practice that views the farm as a cohesive, interconnected living system. It is influenced by lunar and planetary positions.</u>
- <u>Birth Chart (Natal Chart)</u>: <u>A map of where all the planets were in their journey around the Sun, from our vantage point on earth, at the exact moment of one's birth.</u>
- <u>Conjunction</u>: <u>An aspect where two planets are in close proximity to each other in the zodiac, blending and intensifying their energies.</u>
- <u>Element</u>: <u>Each zodiac sign is associated with one of the four elements (Fire, Earth, Air, Water), which represents a fundamental type of energy and approach to life.</u>
- <u>Eclipse</u>: <u>A significant astrological event that occurs when the Sun, Moon, and Earth align, often indicating powerful beginnings or endings.</u>

- **House**: One of the twelve segments of the celestial sphere that represent different areas of life, from the perspective of the Earth.
- **Mercury Retrograde**: A period when Mercury appears to move backward in the sky, traditionally associated with communication, technology, and travel delays or mishaps.
- **Moon Phase**: The lunar cycle from New Moon to Full Moon and back, symbolizing the emotional and intuitive flow of energy.
- **Natal Chart**: See Birth Chart.
- **Opposition**: An aspect in which two planets are across from each other on the zodiac wheel, highlighting areas of potential tension or the need for balance.
- **Planetary Transit**: The movement of the planets through the zodiac signs and houses of one's natal chart, reflecting current influences and experiences.
- **Retrograde**: The apparent backward motion of a planet, indicating a time for reflection and reassessment in the areas governed by the retrograde planet.
- **Sign**: One of the 12 segments of the zodiac, each represented by a symbol and associated with specific characteristics and energies.
- **Square**: An aspect that represents a challenge or obstacle, indicating areas of life that may require effort and determination to integrate or overcome.
- **Trine**: An aspect indicating harmony and flow between the energies of two planets, facilitating ease and natural talent in the areas affected.
- **Zodiac**: The belt of the heavens within about 8° on either side of the ecliptic, divided into 12 equal parts, each named after the constellation that originally occupied the segment.

This glossary is intended to enhance your understanding of the astrological concepts discussed in this book, providing a clearer insight into the profound connection between the stars, planets, and the healing power of hemp.

1. Glossary of Hemp Terms

To complement the celestial insights in "Hemp Horoscopes: Cosmic Insights & Earthly Healing," this glossary defines key terms related to hemp, enriching your understanding of this versatile plant and its role in wellness and spiritual practices.

- **Cannabidiol (CBD)**: A non-psychoactive compound found in cannabis and hemp plants known for its potential therapeutic properties, including reducing anxiety, relieving pain, and improving sleep.
- **Cannabinoids**: Chemical compounds found in cannabis plants that interact with the body's endocannabinoid system to produce a range of effects. CBD and THC are the most well-known cannabinoids.
- **Cannabis**: A plant genus that includes both hemp and marijuana. While both plants are genetically similar, they are regulated and used differently based on their THC content.
- **Endocannabinoid System (ECS)**: A complex cell-signaling system identified in the early 1990s that plays a role in regulating a variety of functions and processes, including sleep, mood, appetite, and memory.
- **Hemp**: A variety of the Cannabis sativa plant species that is grown specifically for industrial use. It contains low levels of THC (below 0.3%) and can be used to produce a variety of products, including textiles, biofuel, food, and health products.
- **Hemp Oil**: An oil extracted from the seeds of the hemp plant, rich in nutrients and fatty acids. It is used in food and beauty products but does not contain CBD or THC.

- **Hemp Seed**: The seed of the hemp plant, which is used to produce hemp oil and hemp protein powder. Hemp seeds are high in protein, fiber, and healthy fatty acids, including omega-3s and omega-6s.
- **Psychoactive**: A chemical substance that changes brain function and results in alterations in perception, mood, consciousness, cognition, or behavior. THC is psychoactive, while CBD is not.
- **Sativa and Indica**: Two primary varieties of cannabis. Sativa strains are known for their energizing effects, while Indica strains are known for their relaxing and sedative effects. Hemp is classified as Cannabis sativa L.
- **Terpenes**: Aromatic compounds found in many plants, including cannabis. They contribute to the plant's smell and flavor and may have therapeutic properties.
- **Tetrahydrocannabinol (THC)**: The main psychoactive compound in cannabis that produces the high sensation. Hemp contains very low levels of THC compared to marijuana.
- **THC-Free**: A term used to describe hemp products that do not contain detectable levels of THC. This is important for individuals who wish to avoid the psychoactive effects of THC or who are concerned about drug testing.
- **Topical**: A product designed to be applied to the skin rather than ingested. Hemp-infused topicals can include creams, balms, and oils, and are often used for localized pain relief or skin conditions.

This glossary aims to provide clarity on the various terms associated with hemp, enhancing your appreciation and understanding of how this ancient plant interacts with both our bodies and the celestial energies discussed throughout the book.

How to access Quality Hemp Products.

Before we get into the other ways you can get quality Hemp Products, check out my Virtual Dispensary for the best hemp infused, Flower, and more:

https://shift.store/sg1fan23477/retail

You will find many great products there, also you will get fast and discreet shipping. All items come from Texas. We do ship international as well.

Tips:

In the burgeoning world of hemp and CBD products, finding high-quality, safe, and effective items can be a challenge. This section provides guidance on navigating the market to ensure you're accessing the best hemp products for your wellness and spiritual practices. Here are key considerations and steps to take when seeking out quality hemp products.

1. Understand Hemp Terminology

Before purchasing, familiarize yourself with terms such as CBD (cannabidiol), THC (tetrahydrocannabinol), full-spectrum, broad-spectrum, and isolate. This knowledge will help you choose products that align with your needs and legal regulations in your area.

2. Research the Source

Quality starts at the source. Look for products made from organically grown hemp that is free from pesticides and herbicides. The best hemp is often sourced from reputable farms in regions known for their hemp cultivation standards, such as certain states in the USA, Canada, and parts of Europe.

3. Check for Third-Party Testing

Reputable manufacturers will have their products tested by independent labs to verify the CBD content and ensure they are free from harmful contaminants like heavy metals, pesticides, and mold. Look for products that provide access to these third-party lab results or certificates of analysis (COAs).

4. Extraction Methods

The method used to extract CBD from hemp affects the quality of the product. CO_2 extraction is considered the gold standard as it preserves the integrity of the CBD and ensures a pure, clean extract without the use of solvents.

5. Read the Label Carefully

A quality hemp product will have clear labeling that includes the amount of CBD per serving, the total CBD content, the suggested use, and a list of ingredients. Avoid products with vague labeling or those that make exaggerated health claims.

6. Understand the Legal Landscape

Hemp's legal status varies by country and, in some cases, by state or province. In many places, hemp-derived CBD products are legal if they contain less than 0.3% THC. Ensure you are familiar with the laws in your area before making a purchase.

7. Start with Reputable Retailers or Direct from Producers

Purchasing directly from the producer's website or from reputable health food stores or dispensaries can increase your chances of getting a high-quality product. These outlets are more likely to provide detailed product information and answer any questions you may have.

8. Seek Recommendations

Personal recommendations from friends or healthcare providers familiar with CBD and hemp products can be invaluable. They can share their experiences with specific brands or products, helping you make informed decisions.

My recommendation is my Virtual Dispensary because I can vouch for it, especially the customers that I have already given samples to love the high quality of the hemp products. The Mushroom sleeping pills I recommend if you have sleeping problems. Go here: https://shift.store/sg1fan23477/retail

9. Be Wary of Price

While the highest price doesn't always mean the best quality, extremely low prices can be a red flag. The production of quality hemp extracts involves significant costs, so be cautious of products that seem too cheap to be true.

10. Start Slow

If you're new to using hemp products, start with a low dose and gradually increase it until you find what works best for you. This approach allows you to gauge the effectiveness of the product and your body's response to it.

Conclusion

Accessing quality hemp products requires diligence, research, and a bit of intuition. By following these guidelines, you can enhance your chances of finding products that are safe, effective, and aligned with your wellness goals. Remember, the journey to finding the right hemp product is personal and may require trying different products before finding the perfect match for your needs.

1. Legal Considerations and Sustainability of Hemp Usage

Being that the Hemp is becoming legalized in the United States, Trump signed into law the 2018 Farm bill allowing the sell of 0.3% Hemp products.

There are many countries where it is still illegal, so do please be careful.

As hemp continues to gain popularity for its wellness and ecological benefits, understanding the legal landscape and sustainability considerations is crucial for consumers and producers alike. This chapter explores the complex legalities surrounding hemp and emphasizes the importance of sustainable practices in its cultivation and usage.

Legal Considerations

Hemp's legal status has evolved significantly in recent years, yet it remains a complex and often confusing area due to varying regulations across different jurisdictions.

- THC Content: Hemp is generally distinguished from marijuana by its low THC content. In many places, hemp is defined as Cannabis sativa L. with a THC content of 0.3% or less by dry weight. Products exceeding this THC threshold are subject to stricter cannabis laws.
- Regulation and Licensing: The cultivation, processing, and sale of hemp and hemp-derived products are

regulated in many countries. Producers often require licenses, and products must meet specific quality and labeling standards.
: **CBD Products**: While hemp-derived CBD products are legal in many regions, the specifics can vary. Some countries allow CBD in cosmetics but not in food products or dietary supplements, and vice versa.
: **International Differences**: The legal status of hemp and CBD varies widely internationally. Before purchasing, using, or traveling with hemp products, verify the laws of your current location and any destinations.

Sustainability in Hemp Cultivation and Usage

Hemp is celebrated not only for its versatility but also for its role in sustainable agriculture and product development.

: **Ecological Benefits**: Hemp cultivation can benefit the environment in several ways. It requires less water and pesticides than many other crops, helps in weed control due to its fast growth, and can improve soil health through phytoremediation.
: **Carbon Sequestration**: Hemp plants are effective at sequestering carbon, making them allies in the fight against climate change. The use of hemp materials in construction and textiles also has a lower carbon footprint compared to traditional materials.
: **Biodegradable and Renewable**: Hemp products, including bioplastics, paper, and textiles, are biodegradable and contribute to reducing waste and pollution.
: **Supporting Local and Organic**: Opting for locally grown, organic hemp supports sustainable practices and reduces

the environmental impact associated with transportation and synthetic inputs.

Ethical and Social Considerations

The hemp industry's growth presents opportunities to address social and ethical issues, including:

- Fair Trade and Labor Practices: Supporting companies that adhere to fair trade principles and provide safe, fair working conditions is crucial.
- Community Impact: The hemp industry can positively impact local communities through job creation and economic development, especially in regions affected by the decline of traditional agriculture or manufacturing.

Conclusion

Navigating the legal and sustainability aspects of hemp usage is essential for making informed decisions that align with personal values and the well-being of the planet. By staying informed about the evolving legal landscape, advocating for clear and fair regulations, and prioritizing sustainability and ethical considerations, consumers and producers can contribute to the responsible growth of the hemp industry. This approach ensures that the benefits of hemp extend beyond individual wellness to foster broader environmental health and social equity.

Conclusion: Weaving the Cosmic Tapestry with Hemp

As we close this exploration of "Hemp Horoscopes: Cosmic Insights & Earthly Healing," we reflect on the profound interconnectedness of the cosmos and hemp—a relationship that spans millennia, bridging the ancient with the modern, the celestial with the terrestrial. This journey has illuminated the ways in which the movements of the planets and the cycles of the moon can harmonize with the healing virtues of hemp, guiding us towards greater well-being, balance, and self-discovery.

The narrative we've woven together is one of unity and synergy. Just as the stars and planets move in a delicate dance through the sky, so too does hemp grow and thrive in response to the rhythms of the natural world. This parallel reminds us that we are not separate from the cosmos or the Earth but are intrinsically connected to the vast web of life. In recognizing this connection, we open ourselves to the healing potential that lies in aligning with these cosmic forces.

Astrology offers a lens through which to view our lives, providing insights and guidance that can help us navigate our path with greater awareness and intention. When combined with the therapeutic properties of hemp, we find a powerful tool for personal growth and healing. Each zodiac sign, with its unique traits and challenges, can find in hemp a companion for the journey, tailored to support and enhance the individual's celestial blueprint.

We encourage you, the reader, to explore the relationship between your astrological sign and hemp. Dive into the rituals and practices suggested within these pages, and experiment with the hemp products that resonate with your cosmic influences. Whether you're seeking physical healing, emotional balance, or spiritual growth, allow the synergy of the stars and this remarkable plant to guide you.

As you embark on this journey, remember that the exploration of astrology and hemp is deeply personal and ever-evolving. What works for one may not work for another, and the true measure of success is how these practices enhance your well-being and enrich your life. Stay curious, remain open to the mysteries of the universe, and embrace the adventure that awaits.

In uniting the wisdom of the cosmos with the healing power of hemp, we find a path to holistic well-being that honors both our individuality and our connection to the greater whole. May this book serve as a compass on your journey, guiding you to deeper health, harmony, and understanding. Under the vast, starlit sky, let us weave our own unique tapestry of healing, supported by the ancient wisdom of astrology and the nurturing power of hemp.

<u>Resources:</u>

This section provides a curated list of resources for those interested in delving deeper into the subjects of astrology and hemp. While the content of "Hemp Horoscopes: Cosmic Insights & Earthly Healing" is drawn from a broad base of knowledge and practice, the resources listed below offer pathways for further exploration, enabling readers to expand their understanding and integrate these insights into their daily lives.

Bibliography of Referenced Works

Please note, for the purpose of this guide, the bibliography is conceptual and should be expanded upon with specific titles relevant to the topics of astrology and hemp as they pertain to personal growth, wellness, and the intertwining of these ancient practices.

1. "The Complete Guide to Astrology: Understanding Yourself, Your Signs, and Your Birth Chart" by Louise Edington
2. "The Art of Hemp: The History and Techniques of Using Hemp" by Jen Hobbs
3. "Astrology for Wellness: Star Sign Guides for Body, Mind & Spirit Vitality" by Monte Farber and Amy Zerner
4. "CBD: A Patient's Guide to Medicinal Cannabis--Healing without the High" by Leonard Leinow and Juliana Birnbaum

5. "Moonology: Working with the Magic of Lunar Cycles" by Yasmin Boland
6. "The Astrology of You and Me: How to Understand and Improve Every Relationship in Your Life" by Gary Goldschneider
7. "Hemp Bound: Dispatches from the Front Lines of the Next Agricultural Revolution" by Doug Fine
8. "Llewellyn's Complete Book of Astrology: The Easy Way to Learn Astrology" by Kris Brandt Riske

Recommended Reading and Websites for Further Exploration

Astrology:

- Astro.com: An extensive resource for free horoscopes, natal chart interpretations, and an astrological community.
- Café Astrology (cafeastrology.com): Offers a wealth of information on astrology, including free reports, charts, and interpretations.
- "The Inner Sky" by Steven Forrest: A compelling introduction to the practice of evolutionary astrology.
- Astrology Zone by Susan Miller (astrologyzone.com): Monthly horoscopes, educational materials, and life and love advice based on astrological signs.

Hemp and CBD:

- Project CBD (projectcbd.org): A non-profit organization dedicated to promoting and publicizing research into the medical uses of CBD and other components of the cannabis plant.

- "The Emperor Wears No Clothes" by Jack Herer: A foundational book on the history and potential of hemp as a resource.
- Ministry of Hemp (ministryofhemp.com): Offers guides, product reviews, and the latest news in the hemp industry.
- NORML (norml.org): Advocacy group with resources on legal issues surrounding cannabis and hemp.

Combining Astrology and Hemp:

- While specific resources that directly combine astrology and hemp are rarer, engaging with communities on platforms such as Reddit, forums dedicated to astrology or holistic healing, and social media groups can provide personal insights, shared experiences, and innovative practices that bridge these subjects.

Note to Readers

As the landscape of astrology and hemp continues to evolve, new resources, research, and communities emerge. We encourage readers to seek out the latest information and stay connected to both fields' growing bodies of knowledge. Remember, the journey into astrology and hemp is deeply personal and infinitely rich, offering endless opportunities for growth, healing, and discovery.

Message from the Author:

I hope you enjoyed this book, I love astrology and knew there was not a book such as this out on the shelf. I love metaphysical items as well. Please check out my other elven books:

-Life of Government Benefits

-My life of Hell

-My life with Hydrocephalus

-Red Sky

-World Domination:Woman's rule

-World Domination:Woman's Rule 2: The War

-Life and Banishment of Apophis: book 1

-The Kidney Friendly Diet

-The Ultimate Hemp Cookbook

-Creating a Dispensary(legally)

-Cleanliness throughout life: the importance of showering from childhood to adulthood.

Check out my Virtual dispensary for all your hemp needs: https://shift.store/sg1fan23477/retail

If you want solar for your home go here: https://www.harbotsolar.live/apophisenterprises/

Instagrams: @apophis_enterprises, @hempkingdom2024, @apophisbookemporium, @apophisfashion, @apophisscardshop

Twitter: @apophisenterpr1, Tiktok:@apophisenterprise

Youtube: @sg1fan23477

Milton Keynes UK
Ingram Content Group UK Ltd.
UKHW040110160324
439374UK00001B/102